Homosexuality and the Bible

Mark Bonnington

Tutor in Biblical Studies (New Testament),
Cranmer Hall, St John's College, Durham

Bob Fyall

Tutor in Biblical Studies (Old Testament),
Cranmer Hall, St John's College, Durham and
Minister of Claypath United Reformed Church

GROVE BOOKS LIMITED
RIDLEY HALL RD CAMBRIDGE CB3 9HU

Contents

1. Being Biblical 3

2. Being Human 7

3. Being Holy 11

4. Being Open 15

5. Being Honest 18

6. Being Practical 24

Preface

This is the first booklet in a new Grove series. Like all Grove booklets, it does not claim to be the last word on its subject, but aims to make a timely contribution to the debate. A consideration of the biblical material is only one part of the church's discussion of the issue of homosexuality, and this booklet should be read in conjunction with Ethical Study 101 *Debating Homosexuality* and Pastoral booklet 38 *No Gay Areas: the Pastoral Care of Homosexual Christians*.

This has not been an easy booklet to write. The issues at stake are very close to home for many who will read it, either because of their personal situation or because they work to minister to those it most directly affects. We have tried to be honest in our arguments without having the space or time to go into all the details of a complex debate. Our conclusions are 'traditional' ones, that will not be popular with many in the church or in our society. We believe that we do no-one any favours by watering down the strenuous demands of the gospel. But we also believe that those strenuous demands find us all wanting in different ways. The glory of the gospel is the forgiveness that we all have in Christ and the hope of new life that we find in him.

As a joint effort we are both happy to own the whole, but you might like to know that Mark wrote chapters 1, 4 and 5, Bob wrote chapters 2 ad 3, and chapter 6 was so pulled about that it can only be described as a joint effort. Mark worked with the Grove Biblical group on editing the whole.

Biblical quotations are from the NRSV unless otherwise stated.

The Cover Illustration is by Peter Ashton

First Impression September 1996
ISSN 1365-490X
ISBN 1 85174 326 X

1

Being Biblical

The Big Little Issue of Homosexuality in the Church

One of the few things that is agreed in the debate over homosexuality within the church is that it is a controversial issue.[1] Views are polarized with both the traditionalists on one side and the revisionists on the other increasingly strident in their arguments. The Church of England in particular is still licking its wounds from the divisive issue of the ordination of women. It now finds itself on the precipice of potentially greater acrimony in the debate over homosexuality.

Irenically inclined believers want to play the issue down. All agree that Scripture itself does not have much explicit to say on the subject—measured by the number of relevant texts it is hardly a major focus of biblical concern. Many suggest that the homosexuality debate is rather far from the centre of gravity of the traditional evangelical concerns for Scripture, preaching, mission and discipleship.

Others are not so sure. Arguments from (near) silence are notoriously dangerous. Some take the presence of debate on homosexuality as indicative of just how far the church has moved from biblical assumptions about Christian sexual behaviour. Some in the churches think that such movement is a good thing, others that it is bad, many that it is simply inevitable. Both revisionists and traditionalists might argue from different perspectives that it is precisely Scripture, mission and discipleship that are at stake. Both believe that they know the best way forward for the church in its attempt to communicate the faith to the modern world. Meanwhile, church authorities craft carefully balanced statements in an effort to keep everyone on board.

Standing at the Crossroads

The issue of homosexuality will not go away and not simply because those with 'strong views' or 'deeply held convictions' will not let it. The debate over homosexuality stands at the crossroads of many other issues which are close to the heart of contemporary evangelical consciousness. There are at least three reasons why this little issue is such a big issue for the church. The first has to do the encounter of contemporary evangelicalism with society, the second with its encounter with the church and the third its encounter with Scripture.

---

1   Rather than engage is lengthy discussion of the use of the terms homosexual, lesbian and gay the usage here will follow what we take to be roughly the convention of contemporary usage. Homosexual is used as a broader term for those who engage in same-sex sexual activity or who are gay or lesbian. 'Gay' and 'lesbian' describe sex differentiated groups who are romantically or sexually attracted to members of their own sex. Sociological studies which use the plural 'homosexualities' to stress the diversity of ways of construing homosexual behaviour nevertheless recognize the core idea of same-sex sexual contact.

The main impetus for changing attitudes to homosexuality is coming from the world in which we live. Today the general drift under the post-Cold War *Pax Americana* is in a liberalizing direction, stressing individual freedom in ethical matters. This drift has been facilitated and encouraged by material prosperity and technological advance. But few who keep a careful ear to political discussion in social and ethical matters would want to suggest that the libertarian tide cannot go out as well as come in.

Christians usually agree that the church should not be following the world on contemporary issues. Either it should be showing the way or it should be heading in a different direction altogether. Too often the churches are caught in the middle neither resisting convincingly nor leading decisively but reluctantly following the cultural stream. Fundamentally at issue here is the question of mission and the uneasy tension between the Christ-against-culture model of the church, ('a light set on a hill') and a Christ-and-culture model of the church working alongside people. Those whose preference is for the latter 'incarnational' model also tend to have greater sympathy for secular norms of behaviour. As the divergence between liberal secular attitudes and the traditional teaching of the church widens, Christians are challenged to re-examine the roots of their convictions. Those who argue for a return to stigmatization or criminalization of homosexuals and those who now argue for a revisionist position may both be guilty of following the ethical direction of the changing world rather than the teaching of Scripture.

The Problem of Pastoral Oversight

Secondly the relationship between evangelicals and the church as a whole is changing. Evangelicalism is growing rapidly, but with this growth come tensions. Evangelicals are now more aware of their own internal diversity. The strength of contemporary evangelicalism is also placing evangelicals in positions of ecclesiastical influence and pastoral responsibility in larger numbers than ever before this century. The pastoral dilemmas raised by the existence of a minority of homosexuals in the church are highlighted as greater openness and publicity do their work. Meanwhile, finding themselves pastorally responsible in some churches for those of other traditions, evangelical church leaders have to show themselves able to exercise appropriate pastoral care and discipline whilst trying to remain true to their evangelical roots and exercise collegial responsibility. This is a stern challenge (if not an impossible task) particularly in churches, like the Church of England, which contain a significant liberal group who are theologically predisposed to the greater acceptance of homosexuality in the church. Although evangelicalism and homosexuality have traditionally been seen as strange bedfellows, greater influence and responsibility has left evangelicals having to face the struggles of exercising sensible and effective pastoral oversight.

The Complexities of Applying Scripture

Thirdly, using Scripture has become more difficult. Over the last thirty years there has been a something of a rapprochement between those in the church for whom the Bible is central and academic biblical scholarship. This has made evangelicals aware of the labyrinthine complexities of scholarly discussion on almost any biblical subject. As a result old certainties often disappear, submerged beneath an ocean of detailed discussion.

Subjects on which Scripture has little explicit to say, like homosexuality, cause us to lean more heavily on considerations from other sources. Tradition, reason and experience can be made to carry great weight. Less obviously relevant passages and patterns in Scripture are also brought to bear. But, most significantly, in the last 20 years evangelicals have discovered the study of hermeneutics—the conscious analysis of the act of interpreting and applying the biblical texts. This has broadened, deepened but also complicated the apparently simple matter of making sense of and applying Scripture. The crisis over homosexuality in the church is a test case over the Bible itself, and how we can make it speak in a modern world that is often hostile to its most explicit statements on a subject.

A Starting Point?

The ongoing task of hermeneutics in the church is to point us to an ethical and godly way of interpreting Scripture. This question of what counts as a 'good' interpretation runs right through discussion of the Bible's approach to homosexuality. An interpretation might be judged 'good' according to whether, for example, it fits with the tradition of the church on homosexuality, or whether it reflects the author's original meaning, or whether it reflects a consensus in the church, or whether it is good or liberating for those the interpretation most affects (in this case gays and lesbians), or whether it makes sense of the whole canonical context of Scripture, or to what extent it impedes or facilitates the mission of the church. Prior choices, often implicit, of what makes an interpretation 'good,' can decisively affect what we make of biblical material. More often than not an interpreter's presuppositions are only clear at the end of the process of interpretation.

We would all like to be able to settle on an interpretation which could be called 'good' from all of these perspectives. But the biblical texts are not infinitely flexible. Evangelicals are not tied to a single approach to biblical interpretation, but they emphasize the importance of seeing themes in the context of the whole of Scripture, taking each text seriously in its own right, discovering the original meaning, and keeping the life, death and resurrection of Christ central. The view set out in this booklet relates homosexuality to major themes of Scripture: creation, incarnation and final redemption. In particular these themes are all integrally related to the major biblical theme of the body.

Body Language

Bodies are important in biblical theology. Scripture tells us that when God created Adam he formed his *body* first from the dust of the earth and then he breathed life into him (Gen 1.7). Much of OT law centres on regulating bodily life. Christian faith has at its heart the incarnation—Christ's sharing the life of our fleshly *bodies*. Indeed Paul tells us that at the heart of the gospel are three things that happened to Christ's *body*—that Christ died, he was buried and he was raised again on the third day (1 Cor 15.3-4). When through baptism believers share in Christ's death, burial and resurrection they not only undergo the spiritual transformation of having their hearts sprinkled clean but they also have their *bodies* washed (Heb 10.22). So too in the bread of the Lord's Supper we remember Christ's broken *body*. Paul calls our *bodies* members of Christ and temples of the Holy Spirit (1 Cor 6.15, 19), and life in the church can simply be described as life in the *body* of Christ.

The Christian hope is hope for personhood not as some ephemeral soul but in the *body*. Judgment will be according to the deeds done in the *body* (2 Cor 5.10). Jesus taught us that we should fear the one who can destroy both *body* and soul in hell (Matt 10.28). Christians hope for the Day when their *bodies* will share the resurrection of Christ himself—we await the redemption of our *bodies* (Rom 8.23). Because our bodies are created by God, indwelt by the Holy Spirit and will be redeemed on that last great Day they have dignity and value; what we do with them is important.

Modern Preoccupations

Our modern society also has much to say about bodies, though its preoccupations have a rather different focus from that of Scripture. By and large it has developed ancient Greek thinking about the body which valued exercise, agility, strength and the beauty of the human form—epitomized in the modern revival of the Olympic games. In its interest in health, strength and beauty the Western world today places the medical, athletic and aesthetic aspects of bodily existence at the top of its concerns. Both the sleek athlete who tunes the body to peak performance and the couch potato who indulges its every whim are ample testimony to today's concern for the body. By contrast the concerns of the Bible with the body are more ethical, eschatological and theological. The cry of Scripture is neither 'health and beauty' nor 'eat, drink and be merry' but God-related: 'Glorify God in your body' (1 Cor 6.20).

Concern for the body has shaped biblical thinking on both sexuality in general and homosexuality in particular. The debate is about bodily acts because God is as concerned with what we do with our bodies as he is with our attitudes and how we think. Because our bodies are God's creation, our expressions of human sexuality in sexual behaviour are to reflect the divine intention. Because we are his people who are indwelt by the Holy Spirit and form Christ's body we are to be a holy people, reflecting a holy God. Because our bodies are also to be redeemed we are to live in a way that will make us fit for the rewards of the coming kingdom.

2

Being Human

One argument frequently urged against a simplistic use of the Bible to condemn homosexual behaviour is that similar arguments have been used to justify slavery, exploitation of women, discrimination against black people and anti-Semitism. It is argued that a more sophisticated hermeneutic would lead us to see that to use the Bible in this way is a similarly reactionary and discreditable enterprise. It is to the biblical material that we now turn.

Two Revisionist Strategies

Writers who argue that a revisionist view can be reconciled with Scripture tend to proceed in one of two ways. On the one hand some argue that parts of Scripture are indeed hostile to homosexual activity, but that these are the flawed and invalid ideas which must be judged and found wanting by other parts of Scripture.[2] A different approach begins with a high view of the authority of Scripture and still concludes that the Bible is compatible with homosexual activity.[3]

What both groups of writers have in common is their emphasis that we should not take single texts in isolation. These must be seen in the 'canonical context' of the whole of the text ('canon') Scripture. Their relation to the culture of their time must be examined carefully to avoid inappropriate comparisons between contemporary lifestyles and very different biblical patterns. This is quite right, and so before analysing specific texts we shall examine Genesis 1 and 2 from which all subsequent teaching on relationships springs. These are foundational texts not only because they are directly quoted throughout Scripture, but because their imagery and theology are woven into the whole fabric of the Bible.

Creation Principles

Genesis 1.26-2.25 is an exploration of what it means to be a human being created in the image of God. It is striking that the verb *bara'*—'to create' (1.1, 21) is employed climactically three times in 1.26-27. *Bara'* is only ever used with God as subject and implies a distinct and special act on God's part. This is complemented by the use of *yatsar* (create) in 2.7, a word used of humans as well as God and suggesting the skilful artistic activity of the potter. Humans, as God's image, are both different from creation and part of it.[4]

---

2 A good example of this view is *Just Good Friends* by Elizabeth Stuart (Mowbray, 1995)—see for example pp 14-25 and pp 143-176.
3 A powerful advocate of this view is Michael R Vasey in *Evangelical Christians and Gay Rights* (Grove Ethical Studies No 80, Nottingham: Grove Books, 1991)—esp pp 7-16 and more recently in *Strangers and Friends* (Hodder & Stoughton, 1995—hereafter just 'Vasey') esp pp 113-140.
4 Useful discussions of 'image' and 'likeness' can be found in V P Hamilton, *The Book of Genesis* (NICOT, 1990) pp 131-150; and G J Wenham, *Genesis* (Word, 1987) pp 26-33.

The arrangement of Genesis 1 and 2 focuses attention first on the reality of the being of God, a God who creates and whose creating activity is expressed using a series of active verbs. God *speaks* and that word is life-giving. God *sees*—no mere casual glance but an expression of the origin of all things in his mind and imagination. God *blesses*, and that blessing is the source of all that is good and lovely. Having established right ideas about God, the text goes on to explore what it means to be human, first by theological statement as in 1.26-28, and then in narrative in Chapter 2. This passage is fundamental in understanding what the Bible has to say about human sexuality.

Male and Female Image

The fundamental fact about the divine image is that it is related to both male and female; what we call masculinity and femininity together reflect realities deep in the being of God. They are not social constructs, subject to the mores of changing societies—they are givens of what it means to be human in any place at any time.

So are Genesis 1 and 2 to be taken as the biblical mandate for monogamous marriage? Some writers have argued that this is simply one pattern among a number of options. Alternative social arrangements, such as polygamy, extended family and cohabitation, may also be evident in Scripture.[5] However, just because something happened and is reported does not mean that it is thereby approved. Indeed the flow of the biblical revelation suggests something very different.

That most notorious polygamist, Solomon, is castigated for both physical and spiritual adultery (1 Kings 11.2ff) and an explicit link is made between the two. A similar emphasis is powerfully presented in Ezekiel 28 where the infidelity of Israel is seen in terms of breaking the covenant which leads directly to the judgment of the Exile. Perhaps the most poignant example is the entire book of Hosea, where physical and spiritual adultery is explored on both divine and human levels. Hosea enshrines the centrality of monogamous marriage.

Becoming One Flesh...

This is reinforced when we turn to an exploration of 'they become one flesh' (Genesis 2.24), also echoed in Ephesians 5.31. Wenham comments: 'It affirms that just as blood relations are flesh and bone, so marriage creates a similar kinship between man and wife.'[6] Paul uses the expression in 1 Corinthians 6.16 to describe someone having sexual relations with a prostitute. Although being 'one flesh' involves much more than genital activity, that activity has awesome significance and outside the union of a loving and committed relationship still carries fundamental consequences.

The Genesis narrative implies that the basic social unit of old Israel was the extended family with all its complex ties and commitments. Yet a particular kind

5   See Stuart p 166 and Vasey pp 115-118.
6   Wenham p 71.

of union is still given an overriding significance: 'Therefore a man leaves his father and mother and clings to his wife' (Gen 2.24). The newly-weds might indeed remain in the same 'homestead' but within that, and notwithstanding their wider responsibilities to the extended family and the whole community, there is an exclusive and unshareable relationship between this man and this woman. That is the pattern affirmed throughout the Bible because of its reflection of the life of God himself. The centrality of monogamous marriage is established in a society in which the community rather than the individual is central—a further powerful pointer to its general applicability across cultures.

...Being in Christ

This metaphor is taken up in Ephesians 5.22-33 and applied to the exclusive commitment of Christ and the church which is reflected in human marriage. In the surrounding verses various relationships are assessed in the light of the gospel and an appropriate lifestyle presented. As is common in the Pauline letters, general exhortations about inner and outward holiness (4.17 to 5.20) are crystallized in a number of relationships.

The 'one flesh' of the heterosexual marriage relationship corresponds to being 'in Christ,' one of the favourite Pauline terms for a Christian. All relationships in this section—those with others, Christians or not (4.25-5.13), parents and children (6.1-4), masters and slaves (6.5-9)—are 'in the Lord' and governed by our relationship to him and thus are to be characterized by love and respect. However, only the marriage relationship in its mystery reflects the actual nature both of God himself and of humans who are his image.

Friendship

Does same-sex friendship equally provide a paradigm for the relationship between God and his people?[7] Scripture does recognize and value strong same sex friendships—Ruth and Naomi, David and Jonathan, Paul and Timothy. But there is no evidence that these strongly emotional relationships had anything like a 'homo-erotic' element.[8] David does indeed say of Jonathan, 'Your love to me was wonderful, passing the love of women,' and Saul is furious at the 'shame' of Jonathan's friendship for David (1 Sam 2.30). However, the context makes it plain that the shame is political rather than sexual: 'For as long as the son of Jesse lives upon the earth, neither you nor your kingdom shall be established'(v31).

There is simply no evidence of friendship being used as a controlling image in the way that marriage is seen as a human expression of the love of the Trinity. Friendship is a good and gracious gift to sweeten human community and can be an element within a sexual relationship. Song of Songs 5.16 expresses this beautifully, where the woman says of her lover: 'This is my beloved and this is my friend.' The woman is affirming that the raptures of early love will be maintained

---

7   See for example Vasey, pp 120-124, 233-237.
8   The expression is used by Vasey—eg p 121.

9

because the person she has married is also her best friend. But same-sex friendship in and of itself does not have the paradigmatic significance of the marriage relationship.

Fruitfulness

Another element in this rich picture of what it is to be human is defined in the command 'Be fruitful and multiply' (Genesis 1.28). One of the purposes of marriage, and one of the elements of the image, is the bearing of children. Childbearing is not associated with fallenness. It is there in the unfallen world. There is no hint here that sexuality is wrong; rather the concern is to set it in its proper context.

Bearing children is the natural result of the kind of union envisaged in Genesis 1 and exemplified in Genesis 2. It is not, however, in the fallen world an inevitable result. The curse involving child-bearing in Genesis 3.16 is not a charter for a brutal chauvinism but a description of the realities of a fallen world. Similarly childlessness may be a consequence of living in such a world. What the Genesis passages are teaching is that the bearing of children is normally an integral part of the marriage covenant. The fundamental union of a woman and a man is the biblical context for the bearing and rearing of children.

Human families have a central role in the divine purposes for humanity. This becomes a major theme of later parts of Genesis where the importance of children is emphasized in different ways in, for example, the stories of Cain and Abel and of Abraham. This is not to argue for an idolizing of the 'nuclear family.' Jesus does indeed warn of the dangers of loving family more than God—but that is in the context of a radical call to discipleship in which loving anything more than God is seen as a hindrance to the life of faith. The biblical way is to see a loving marriage and family as an anticipation of heaven rather than a substitute for it.

Genesis 1 and 2 emphasize the givenness of maleness and femaleness, and of the conjugal heterosexual family. As part of the created order these are trans-historical and trans-cultural and is emphasized throughout the OT and into the NT. For the revisionist case to stand, there would need to be demonstrated a similar positive affirmation of homosexuality (not simply same-sex friendships) as a controlling model for God's relationship with the universe and humankind.

3

Being Holy

'If homosexuality is wrong because the Bible says so, you must equally condemn eating prawns and pork. And, in any case, why don't you press for the death penalty for homosexuals since the Bible advocates that as well?'

This question summarizes the view that the prohibition of same-sex activity in Leviticus is time-conditioned and cannot simply be used as a norm for sexual behaviour.[9] Having explored the fundamental nature of the male/female complementarity in the Genesis narrative and its echoes throughout Scripture, we must now look at the Leviticus texts which appear to rule out homosexual acts. The relevant texts are:

'Do not lie with a man as one lies with a woman, that is detestable' (Leviticus 18.22).
'If a man lies with a man as one lies with a woman, both of them must be put to death; their blood will be on their own heads' (Leviticus 20.13).

To avoid the danger of selectivity, this chapter will examine the context of the texts, offer an exegesis of 18.22, tackle the issues raised in the comments above and finally make some brief observations on the relationship of holiness, law and grace.

The Context

These texts are not isolated and arbitrary snippets; they are part of a world view presented in Leviticus and the Pentateuch that derives principles for living from allegiance to Yahweh. He is Lord of creation and history and not merely a local 'godlet' of Israel. In that context, Leviticus is presented as words of the Lord 'from the Tent of Meeting,' the place where the glory of the Lord is visibly encountered. Yet, significantly, the glory cloud is not confined there but accompanies the people on their pilgrimage; the words from the glory are valid for the whole journey.

Within Leviticus itself the two texts occur in the so-called 'Holiness Code' (chapters 17-26) which immediately follows a similar block of material sometimes called the 'purification code' (chapters 11-16) containing the regulations on prawns and pork. Both these sections are bracketed with the assertion that they are the words of Yahweh (11.1 and 16.34; 17.1 and 26.46). The chapter that particularly concerns us has a fairly lengthy introduction (18.1-5) and an extended conclusion (18.24-29).

---

9 See A Sullivan, *Virtually Normal* (Picador, 1995) pp 27-28.

The social reality envisaged in Leviticus 18 is the 'father's house,' the extended family. This was the basic social unit of ancient Israel to which an individual related and where several generations lived near to each other.[10]

The Texts

Leviticus 18.22 is a crucial passage because, as Boswell points out, this is 'the only place in the Old Testament where homosexual acts *per se* are mentioned.'[11] Sociological and anthropological studies, while valuable, are of secondary importance here. Arguments about the kinds of homosexuality in very different cultures, while valid in context, are not easy to relate to an understanding of this passage. This text does not condemn a disposition but prohibits same-sex sexual activity. This kind of activity offends the creator, the Lord of history and the covenant-keeping God. It is broad enough to encompass any such act; it is the activity itself, not a particular form of it, which is prohibited.

Boswell argues that there is doubt about the meaning of the phrase 'lie with a man as with a woman.'[12] He maintains that it could refer to temple prostitution rather than homosexual behaviour in general. But this has no support in the passage, which refers to behaviour in the household. Such behaviour is described as *tô`ebah*, a strong term variously translated as 'detestable, abominable, abhorrent.' In Leviticus it tends to refer to the sexual practices of Israel's neighbours. It also occurs in Deuteronomy, Ezekiel and Proverbs and refers to actions and attitudes which are incompatible with the holiness of Yahweh. Simply stated, homosexual activity is not compatible with a lifestyle ordered by loyalty to Yahweh.

Is Leviticus Relevant?

The quotation at the beginning of this chapter sharply raises the question of whether the texts on homosexuality in the OT have anything to say to Christians at all. The issue of how the OT in general—and the law codes in particular—apply to Christians has been debated since the time of the early church. There are three possible approaches.

The first is simply to set aside the whole of the Old Testament in the light of the New. This was advocated in the early church by Marcion, but has never been accepted by the church as an adequate response to the Scriptures that were of

---

10 See Hartley, pp 285-291 for a useful discussion of the family in ancient Israel.

11 J Boswell, Christianity, *Social Tolerance and Homosexuality* (Univ of Chicago Press, 1980) p 100. There is a growing consensus about Genesis 19.1-29 that 'Sodom is not about sodomy' (cf the similar story in Judges 19). The 'men of Sodom' clearly intend to rape Lot's visitors, not realizing that they are angels. This behaviour exemplifies the great wickedness of the city. The fault here is more than inhospitality ('bring them out so that we can be inhospitable to them'!), since it is clear that there is a sexual element (19.5,8) which may be sexual violence or homosexuality. The rejection of the offer of virgins as a substitute indicates that the homosexual element heightens the offence. The story is mentioned elsewhere in Scripture (Deut 29.23-26; Jer 23.14; Ex 16.46-50; 2 Pet 2.6-7; Jude 7). The obscure reference in Jude to 'strange flesh' (sex with angels?) comes closest to identifying the sin of Sodom as homosexuality. The Jewish writers Philo (eg *On Abraham* 133-41) and Josephus (*Ant* 1.200-204) see in the incident violent homosexual behaviour.

12 Boswell, p 101 n 34.

central importance to Jesus and the earliest Christians, be they Jewish or gentile. A modern variation of this approach is to claim that the law codes are 'part of a symbolic system that does not apply to Christians.'[13]

The second approach is to take all of the OT commands as applying to us today. But again, this is unsatisfactory. As the early church came to terms with the impact of the gentile mission, there was a fierce debate as to whether gentiles needed to obey all the Jewish customs (set out in books like Leviticus), or whether there were some central principles and patterns of life that were binding and others that were not. To have adopted the first approach would effectively have been to say that gentiles needed to become Jews before they could become Christians. Instead, we read of the 'apostolic decree' in Acts 15, where the church in Jerusalem decides that the most important matters concerned idolatry, the sanctity of life, and (most pertinent to our discussion) sexual morality (fornication). This leads us to the third possible approach, which is to believe that whilst not all the specific commands of the OT are binding on Christians, there are patterns and principles that transcend the context in which the law was given. Thus it is that Mark makes clear to his (probably Roman) readers that they need not obey the food purity laws (Mark 7.19). And Paul takes up this principle in his declaration, again to the Romans, that 'the kingdom of God is not a matter of eating and drinking' (Rom 14.17).

How can we tell which patterns and principles are binding on us, and which are only rooted in the context of the Exodus and the settling of the land? There is not space here to give a systematic answer to this question. But I do want to argue a central point: where a command is grounded in a creation principle, and where it is taken up unequivocally in the NT, we can be confident that this is a lasting pattern for Christians.

The prohibition on homosexual acts is related to the right ordering of family relationships which is reflected paradigmatically in the teaching on male-female union in Genesis 1-2. In the next chapters we will also see how it is taken up in the NT. In contrast, the food laws are not rooted in creation; indeed, in Genesis 1 God declares that all his creation is good. (A similar point could be made regarding slavery, whatever form it takes.) And the death penalty for same-sex acts (in 20.13) is the response to a breaking of the law in a particular context—that of desert wandering and conquest. In the NT, this is substituted by the offer of forgiveness in Christ, or the alternative of eschatological judgment (in 1 Cor 6.9). There are numerous examples of OT commands or prohibitions that still have force for Christians, but where the original sanction for disobedience has been set aside.

To Be Holy

Holiness is not so much a characteristic of God as the essence of his nature. The heart of the Holiness Code is summed up in Leviticus 19.2—'Be holy because I, the Lord your God, am holy.' Thus persons, places and activities are holy only

---

13 Vasey, p 126.

in relation to him. According to Genesis 1 and 2, homosexual activity does not reflect the nature of God. However attractive or effective in other respects the people practising may be, they cannot therefore be regarded as holy.

But what about God's gracious welcome of sinners revealed in Jesus 'who welcomes sinners and eats with them?' (Luke 15.2). Scripture does not present a contrast between the God and Father of our Lord Jesus Christ and Yahweh of the OT. The Mosaic law was a gift of grace; grace should not be too readily contrasted with law. It is grace which gives law as a light to guide us in the fallen world and to drive us into the arms of that love by which alone the law can be obeyed.

The call to be holy is echoed and reaffirmed in the NT. 1 Peter 1.15-16 specifically repeats the call to holiness of Leviticus 19.2. The acceptance of sinful people by God is not a licence to continue in ungodliness but a call to holiness.

4

Being Open

The idea of 'openness' is important in many sections of the church today. Few people want a reputation for unthinking dogmatism. The destructive and antagonizing effects of reflex responses and entrenched views are all too evident in the contemporary world, whether in religious fundamentalism or strident 'political correctness.' The concern of the church with openness centres around both how it conducts its internal theological discussions and, more vitally, how it can facilitate effective mission. What is true Christian openness?

Vasey (pp 58-63) has argued that the approach of the church to gay people should be characterized by the 'method of grace.' He is keen not to emphasize sexual sins above others. He rightly stresses the instructive role of grace, and suggests that grace points to 'some pastoral pragmatism' and implies some 'penitent tolerance of some imperfection in...sexual matters'.[14]

Sex and Grace

Sexual sins, like all sins are to be taken seriously, the more so because they involve our bodies, which belong to God, are members of Christ, and are the place the Holy Spirit indwells. Sexual sin is a sin against our own bodies, but also involves Christ himself. Paul teaches that in sexual relations with a prostitute, Christ himself is joined to a prostitute (1 Cor 6.15-20). To engage in homosexual intercourse might similarly be said to be equivalent to making Christ himself engage in a homosexual act.

Grace is indeed the right context for growing in the faith. But grace must retain a cutting edge of the radical call to discipleship if it is not to lapse into cheap grace and easy toleration. Jesus himself embodies this outlook in his own ministry.

He refuses to play the part of judge in the story of the attempted lynching of the woman caught in adultery (John 8.53-9.12), but uses the universal sinfulness of her accusers as a tool to defuse the situation. In the absence of the required two witnesses against her, Jesus himself refuses to pronounce the condemnation to death required under the law. Rather he sends her away—leaving her with the instruction and the responsibility not to sin again. Jesus' actions may show a change in attitude to the penalty for adultery but not to the definition of sexual sin.

---

14 The choice of 1 Thess 4.1-8 as an example of this 'method of grace' is admirable and courageous but a little odd (Vasey p 60). The passage clearly addresses those whom Paul regards as already successful in living to please God (4.1), consists mainly of a number of exhortations and requests, does not mention grace and includes Paul's solemn warning that 'the Lord is an avenger in all these things' (4.6).

Table Fellowship

In his table-fellowship Jesus shows his radical social openness to the high and low of his society. He ate happily with his opponents the Pharisees, the rich and collaborative tax-collectors and with those 'sinners' in Israel who did not keep the law.[15] But repentance is also a consistent theme in the stories of Jesus' table-fellowship. In the house of Levi Jesus explains that his task in eating with tax-collectors and sinners is to call them to repentance (Luke 5.29-32 cf Luke 19.1-10). Jesus' teaching stirred up trouble when eating at the houses of Pharisees (Luke 11.37-41; 14.1-25). The parables of the lost indicate both the centrality of the call to repentance involved in Jesus' table-fellowship and his criticism of those who think that 'sinners' had not repented or could not repent (Luke 15). However comfortable Jesus may or not have felt in social situations which others considered dangerous or inappropriate for a teacher, it is clear that his hosts did not always find Jesus a compliant and affable dinner-guest. What was attractive about Jesus was not his assimilation to the culture of those he came into close contact with. Rather it was the closeness of one so different that offered sinners a sign of hope.[16] Even if Jesus would have felt at home in a gay bar, it is not so clear that those in the gay bar would have felt so comfortable with what he had to say whilst he was there.

Judgment and Judgmentalism

Jesus taught that we should 'not judge that [we] may not be judged' (Matt 7.1) and Christians are rightly wary of being 'judgmental.' But Paul taught that judgment was an essential preparation for the destiny of the believers (1 Cor 5.9-6.11 'we are to judge angels'), to be exercised by the community and within the community. Eschatological judgment therefore points not only to the dangers of judgment but also to the responsibility of preparing for judgment.

Both Jesus (Matt 18.15-20) and Paul (1 Cor 5.1-5, 9-13) taught that there were limits to the forms of behaviour acceptable within the church and that ultimately those who refused to recognize those limits should be excluded.[17] Two elements preserve the church from judgmentalism in its exercise of discipline. The first is the communal dimension of the task. Correction should begin with the personal word of admonition but ultimately it is the responsibility not of individuals but of the whole Christian community to exercise appropriate discipline. Secondly, the aim of Christian discipline is always redemptive. Discipline is never used because of sin itself, but because of failure to repent and strive for a change of heart

---

15 Saying exactly who the 'sinners' of Jesus ministry were is difficult, but they were probably apostate Jews who made no attempt to keep the Jewish law. The idea that their sins, which Jesus apparently accepted as such (Luke 7.47-50), were exclusively or mainly sexual is quite unproven (Vasey p 59, for example, turns the woman sinner of Luke 7.36-50 into a prostitute).

16 Paul too was quite prepared to share the radical openness of table fellowship with gentile 'sinners' (Gal 2.11-14) without compromising on the demands involved in obeying the truth (Gal 5.7-26).

17 It has been pointed out that 'Where two or three are gathered in my name, there am I amongst them' (Matt 18.20) is not for our encouragement at badly attended prayer-meetings but is set in the context of church discipline.

and life. The aim is to save the sinner from the sin, and prepare for the day of judgment (1 Cor 5.5). The judgment of the church is only provisional; ultimately God will judge us all. Those who correct in the name of Christ do so in the humbling knowledge that there will be a day when they themselves will stand before the judge of all. We do well to heed Paul's exhortation: 'If any one is detected in any transgression, you…should restore such a one in a spirit of gentleness' (Gal 6.1).

True Openness

True Christian openness has two dimensions. First it distinguishes between what is expected of those within the Christian community and those beyond it. This is grounded theologically in the very idea of salvation. God's free offer of grace and forgiveness deals with human sin and begins in us the process of redemption which will culminate in the final consummation. We are not yet perfect but we have already begun the process of transformation. The church is called to be a living witness to this truth. Secondly, in the openness of Christians to those outside the church, there is to be a radical disjunction between the degree of social openness, which is to be great, and the degree of ideological openness, which is much less. This perspective is rooted in the mission of the church which compels us to engage with those around in order to communicate the gospel. But because it is the *gospel* we must preach—in all its transforming power and radical demand—engagement with unbelievers cannot be allowed to blunt our commitment to the truth of the gospel.

That is not to say that openness is easy to maintain. It may not be possible, nor desirable, to say exactly where the boundaries of the church lie—though most churches have some form of membership or recognition of active fellowship, centring on regular participation in the Communion. There are different views on the purity of the visible church. And not all Christians agree on how much we can or should learn from contemporary society. But whatever the precise shape of the ecclesiastical context in which is must be made to work, the basic shape of biblical thinking on Christian openness is clear. To put it simply, the task of Christian openness is to keep the church in the world and to keep the world out of the church.

5
Being Honest

Paul's Three Texts

There are only three NT texts which deal explicitly with homosexuality and they are all found amongst the Pauline letters. Because of both their explicitness and their significance for the historic tradition of the church, 1 Cor 6.9, 1 Tim 1.10 and especially Rom 1.24-32 bring us to the centre of debate over homosexuality. They stand in the letters of the apostle who wrote in the post-Easter period mainly to gentile believers like us. Despite the difficulties in saying exactly why Paul took over some aspects of this Jewish heritage (like monotheism) and not others (like the food laws) for gentile believers it is quite clear that rejection of the Mosaic law as the basis for Christian ethics did not stop the early Christian communities taking on board very many specific ethical injunctions.

With these texts revisionist approaches have their work cut out to provide a plausible alternative to the historic reading that homosexual activity is not acceptable for Christian believers. The burden of explaining why Paul taught this falls more or less squarely on the Romans passage. Whilst 1 Cor 6.9 and Tim 1.10 demonstrate that Paul assumed that certain forms of homosexual behaviour were wrong, it is in Romans 1 that he gives us greatest insight into his underlying rationale.

A number of complementary revisionist interpretative strategies emerge for interpretation of these texts, including efforts to:

i) *marginalize* the texts by refusing to give them key significance for the debate, arguing for alternative 'starting points' or submerging them under wider exegetical and theological considerations;

ii) *'fuzzify'* the texts by arguing that their meaning is too general or uncertain for definite conclusions to be drawn, so that alternative (revisionist) conclusions are at least possible and part of the acceptable range of readings. On this kind of argument revisionist readings do not have to be right, they only have to be 'not wrong'—they can be unlikely as long as they are possible;

iii) *distance* the texts from the contemporary debate by arguing that the cultural and symbolic context which gave rise to them is too different from our own for the texts to speak with decisive weight today.

Romans 1.24-32: Homosexual Behaviour is 'Revolting'

This passage is part of Paul's argument in the early chapters of Romans to show that all humanity, Jews and gentiles alike, are subject to sin (Rom 2.12, 3.9). After arguing in Chapter 1 for the Jewish commonplace that gentiles are sinners, he turns the rhetorical tables on the smugly approving Jewish listener and argues just as forcefully that Jews too are under sin (Rom 2.1). Neither the covenant sign of circumcision nor the law alter the conclusion that all have sinned and so are in need of the righteousness revealed in Christ (3.21). Whatever we make of the crucial verses in Romans 1.24-27, Hays is right to point out that Paul's rhetorical 'sting' in Romans 2.1-6 warns us all against easy condemnation of others in the light of our own sinfulness and need of God's mercy in the day of judgment.[18] But Schmidt is also right to warn that Paul does 'not throw out the baby of righteousness with the bath water of self-righteousness.'[19]

This is the only biblical passage to mention lesbianism as well as male homosexuality and it highly unusual amongst ancient texts in discussing the two together.[20] The attitude of Paul's contemporary culture to male homosexuality varied.[21] Some, like Plato, condemned it because it was non-procreative; others approved in various circumstances largely depending on the age and relative social status of the participants. Sexual relations between females was regarded uniformly negatively, at least by the male writers whose works we have. Amongst Jews, like the first-century Jewish philosopher Philo, attitudes to all forms of homosexuality were consistently negative. Although many Jewish arguments paralleled those of Greek writers, the underlying Jewish motivation was obvious—the Mosaic law forbade homosexuality.

We can draw two immediate conclusions from the fact that Paul discusses male homosexuality and lesbianism in tandem. First, because Paul includes women he cannot have been thinking of specific sexual acts, like anal intercourse, as the focus of his comments, despite later discussions in the Christian tradition. Secondly, by extending the biblical rejection of male homosexuality to lesbianism Paul shows that he has no interest in the question of the appropriate social status distinctions (or 'power relations') between insertive and receptive partners in male homosexual intercourse which was characteristic of gentile discussions. Paul's rejection of homosexual relations depended not on the type of sexual behaviour, nor the power relationship of the participants, but on the same-sex nature of the relationship.

Failing to Recognize

The thrust of Paul's argument in Romans 1 is an explanation of gentile behaviour in the light of their rejection of God's self-disclosure in creation (1.19-20). The result of this failure of recognition was idolatry—a focus on the created order shown particularly in false worship (1.23), sexual misbehaviour (1.24-27) and all kinds of sin (1.28-32). Hays (p 8) points out that the logic of

---

18 R B Hays, 'Awaiting the Redemption of our Bodies: The Witness of Scripture concerning Homosexuality' in J S Siker (ed), *Homosexuality in the Church* (Westminster John Knox, 1994), p 9.
19 T E Schmidt, *Straight and Narrow?* (IVP, 1995), p 66.
20 V P Furnish, 'The Bible and Homosexuality: Reading the Texts in Context' in Siker (p 28) is quite wrong to suggest that 'there is nothing distinctively Pauline, or even Christian' in what Paul wrote.
21 Schmidt, pp 65-66, gives a brief and readable summary. There is a more extended discussion in D F Greenburg, *The Construction of Homosexuality* (Univ of Chicago Press, 1988) pp 141-160.

Paul's argument makes these things not a provocation of divine wrath but a consequence of God's giving up his creatures to their own futile thinking. The sins of Romans 1.22-32 are symptoms of a root cause—gentile failure to recognize God (1.21-23).

Therefore Paul's comments on homosexuality are part of this wider theme of human failure to recognize or acknowledge the creator. The result of this failure was the terrible divine 'hands-off' (1.24, 26, 28) leaving humankind to their own devices and consequent moral degradation. As Schmidt (p 67) puts it, homosexual acts are quite literally 'revolting, in that they represent a revolt against the created order.'

The Link with Idolatry

Some revisionists have argued that Paul's argument does not imply the rejection of forms of homosexuality which are not specifically linked to idolatry. As a first-century Jew (so the argument goes), the association of homosexuality and paganism was too pervasive for Paul to have been thinking of forms of homosexuality that were separated from a pagan, idolatrous context (so Furnish pp 25-29). Faced with other forms of homosexuality which, because of their ethical or religious qualities, cannot be described as idolatrous, we should recognize the limited nature of Paul's strictures. Modern gays and lesbians do not bow down to lumps of stone; their lives often display Christ-like qualities and many, of course, are Christian believers. Such people are not in view in Romans 1.

Attractive as this line of argument is, it is in danger of turning Paul from a theologian into a naïve social commentator. Paul knew from the Mosaic law the possibility of homosexuality amongst Israelites—since these were the very ones to whom the law was given.

The phrase 'receiving the due penalty for their error' in Romans 1.27 is a reference to legal strictures. The law is obviously in Paul's mind when he condemns the self-justification which is the bedfellow of moral corruption: 'though they know God's decree that those who do such things deserve to die, they not only do them but approve those who practise them' (Rom 1.32). Paul is not thinking here only or mainly about homosexuality, but he does indicate that the penalties imposed by Mosaic law demonstrate divine disapproval of such behaviour.

Paul did not think the law irrelevant to gentiles nor did he take a simplistic view of the moral potential of the gentiles—he could, for example, easily envisage the existence of righteous gentiles (Rom 2.25-29).

Nature and Creation

But the main problem with the revisionist line of argument is the failure to recognize that the core problem expressed in Romans 1 is human failure to acknowledge the creator. This cashes out in three types of failures in creaturely relations: the religious sin of worshipping creatures (1.23-25); the sexual sin of passion for the wrong creatures (1.26-27) and the social sins involved in antagonized relationships with other human creatures (1.29-31).[22] Indeed the whole passage has creation as its context. Although there are no direct quotations from Genesis 1-3, there are allusions (compare 'male' and 'female' in 1.26-7 with Gen 1.27), and in talking about 'nature' Paul is speaking of the divine intention for human sexual relationships expressed in creation.

Particularly relevant to this creation-context is Paul's talk of the 'exchange' of 'natural' intercourse for that 'contrary to nature' (*para phusin*).[23] McNeill argued that Paul could conceive only of perverts, who had homosexual relations whilst having heterosexual desires, not inverts, who had exclusive attraction to their own sex.[24] Paul's talk of 'exchange' (1.26 cf 1.23, 25), however, is not about personal sexual preferences but about the rejection of the divinely ordained order.

Nature and Culture

Plato criticized male homosexuality using the same phrase *para phusin*, meaning by it sexual acts not directed towards procreation (see Republic 5.13; Laws 6.26 b-c). Through terminological coincidence the same idea spread in the Christian tradition particularly under the influence of Augustine. Nature (*phusis*) is a word with a broad range of meanings including 'physical descent' (Gal 2.15) and perhaps something like 'cultural heritage.' Paul uses it variously in Romans itself (2.14,27; 11.21,24). Vasey (pp 133-134) makes much of the parallel of 1 Cor 11.14, noting the use there of both *phusis* and *atimia*, 'dishonour.' He argued that since *phusis* means something culture-specific in Corinthians it does so in Romans and that such an understanding of *phusis* is part of Paul's 'missiological pragmatism.' It is far from clear that Vasey construes Paul's meaning correctly in 1 Corinthians, though it may mean 'social convention' there. But *phusis* was a flexible word with shade of meaning determined by context. Given the creation context of Romans 1 it is clear that here *phusis* is intended by Paul to mean the divine intention expressed in the created order and therefore a trans-cultural, timeless ideal.

Paul's discussion in Romans 1 is a combination of Greek terminology, biblical ideas and his own creative thinking. It is very far from a conventional Jewish or Greek comment on homosexual behaviour. Although he regards same-sex sexual behaviour as sinful, the main point that he is making is that it exemplifies human failure to acknowledge the Creator and his ways in his creation. As such it is part of the evidence for the universal sinfulness of humanity and points us all to our need of salvation in Christ.

---

22 W L Countryman, *Dirt, Greed and Sex* (SCM, 1989) pp 109-113, tries to argue that homosexuality was not a matter of sin but impurity, and so part of an outdated symbolic purity system irrelevant to modern Christianity. But he attempts to make an invalid distinction between sin and impurity and fails to recognize that the context places sexual misbehaviour between the sin of idolatry and social sins.

23 Paul may have taken up this phraseology from popular Greek or Stoic usage, and he used ideas paralleled in Jewish thinking (Ps 106.19-20; Wis Sol 13.1; 14.12,26) see Fitzmyer, *Romans* (Anchor Bible, Geoffrey Chapman, 1993) p 286. It is a mistake to conclude from this that the horizons of his thinking were limited by such ideas—Paul may have used them precisely because they fitted with his own theological framework.

24 McNeill *The Church and The Homosexual* (Sheed, Andrews and McMeel, 1976) pp 55-56.

1 Corinthians 6.9-11: Malakoi *and* Arsenokoitai *Cannot Inherit the Kingdom*

Paul's thinking in 1 Cor 6.9-11 is eschatological—that is, it is to do with the end times and the coming kingdom of God. In verses 9 and 10 he gives a list of ten types of people whose characteristic behaviours will mean their exclusion from the eschatological kingdom. The list includes the Greek words *malakoi* and *arsenokoitai* whose meanings are related to homosexuality.

Malakoi and *arsenokoitai* literally translated mean, respectively, 'soft ones' and 'those that lie with men.' Detailed studies of the ancient texts show that *malakos* could have a broad range of meanings ranging from gentle, through effeminate to a receptive male homosexual.[25] Sandwiched between two other words with sexual connotations it certainly has a sexual meaning. It cannot therefore have as general a meaning as 'loose living' (Vasey p 135) but nor is it likely to have as specific a meaning as 'male prostitute.' Doing justice to both the sexual connotation and the generality of the word leads to the conclusion that it simply means men who make themselves attractive to other men. One explanation is to bracket *malakoi* with *arsenokoitai* and see the two as the receptive and insertive partners in anal intercourse. But such a specific meaning is rendered unlikely by the fact that Paul uses rather general terms.

Meaning and Origin: 1 Tim 1.10–11

Paul's use of the word *arsenokoitai* is the first that we know of in ancient Greek. Although we cannot be sure that Paul invented the word, Wright's suggestion that it emerged in Hellenistic Judaism as a result of the rendering of Lev 18.22 and 20.13 in the Septuagint (the Greek OT that Christians read) is sound.[26] Both the appearance together there of *arsen* (man) and *koite* (bed) to translate the Mosaic ban on those 'who lie with men' and the absence of the term in other Greek writers is a good indication of such an origin.

The word *arsenokoitai* appears again in 1 Tim 1.8-11. Verses 8 and 9 indicate explicitly that the OT law is in view and provides confirmation that Paul and others had Leviticus in view in using the word *arsenokoitai*. Such behaviour is not only contrary to the law but 'to the sound teaching that conforms to the glorious gospel' (1 Tim 1.10-11).

If we needed a simple modern equivalent for *arsenokoitai* then 'men who sleep with other men' would retain both the generality and the euphemistic quality of the word. Arguments that in using *arsenokoitai* Paul must have had a specific cultural model in mind (like pederasts) are dealt a decisive blow with this simple recognition that Paul's categories were Jewish and biblical. Because Leviticus uses the analogy of sex with a woman, the word can be taken as a rather general one for sexual activity between men and cannot be narrowed down to (say) anal intercourse.

---

25 See G D Fee, *1 Corinthians* (NICNT Eerdmans, 1987) pp 243-244.

26 D F Wright, 'Homosexuals or Prostitutes? The Meaning of Arsenokoitai (1 Cor 6.9; 1 Tim 1.10),' *Vigiliae Christianae* 38 (1984) pp 125-53.

Past and Present

In 1 Corinthians 6.9-11 Paul tells us that some of the Corinthians were *malakoi* and *arsenokoitai* before being converted. But he also indicates that their lives had subsequently been transformed as a result of their Christian conversion: 'such were some of you' (verse 11). The sanctifying and justifying work brought about in Christ made it *possible* for such behaviour to be a thing of the past, the conditions of entry for the kingdom made it *necessary* for such behaviour to be a thing of the past.

Paul's exhortation shows that the Corinthian church contained those who, from a Christian point of view, had been morally or religiously depraved before conversion. Corinth can be seen as an excellent example of an open church which accepted people irrespective of their previous moral history. But it was also a community of transformation and expectation where such behaviours were to be left behind not principally because of the 'high' entry requirements of the church but because of the high entry requirements of the eschatological kingdom. For Paul, those who sleep with other men are in just as much danger of exclusion as idolaters, adulterers, thieves or drunkards.

Nevertheless the immediate context of our passage also shows just how seriously Paul took the purity of the church. Six of the ten types of people who Paul says will not inherit the kingdom also appear in the preceding chapter (5.10-11). There Paul lists a number of types of 'brother' to whom the Corinthians should not extend even the most basic form of fellowship—a meal together. It is hard to imagine that Paul would not have expected *malakoi* and *arsenokoitai* to be placed under a similar ban.

To Be Honest

I realize that this exegesis of Paul may be painful for those on the horns of a practical dilemma regarding their sexuality. But if we are to take Scripture seriously then we must be honest about what Paul is saying. Despite the hopeful exegesis of revisionist writers it is clear that all forms of homosexual behaviour are, according to Paul, to be regarded as sinful. But Paul reminds us that all have sinned and are saved not by being 'straight' but by being 'in Christ.'

6
Being Practical

'When the people heard this, they...said to Peter..."What shall we do?"' These words from Acts 2.37 must be at the heart of every attempt to expound the Bible. How does all this translate into action? What are we to be and do as a result of our exposure to Scripture? Throughout this booklet we have emphasized that specific texts relating to homosexual behaviour must be seen not as isolated instructions but as part of biblical teaching on humanity. We must now move from a focus on the moral, ethical and theological issues to the pastoral and political ones of how Scripture guides us on the appropriate attitudes and actions within the Christian community.

'For the grace of God has appeared, bringing salvation to all, training us to renounce impiety and worldly passions, and in the present age to live lives that are self-controlled, upright and godly, while we wait for the blessed hope and the manifestation of the glory of our great God and Saviour, Jesus Christ. He it is who gave himself for us that he might redeem us from all iniquity and purify for himself a people of his own who are zealous for good deeds. Declare these things; exhort and reprove' (Titus 2.11–15).

This passage is quoted in full because it is a remarkably comprehensive and detailed statement about grace and encapsulates the approach of this chapter. The grace revealed in Christ is not genial tolerance but the undeserved divine initiative which is also a means of training and maturing in the faith. The church is therefore a place of transformation and preparation where, by teaching, by exhortation and encouragement, by admonition and discipline and by love, we help one another in our walk of holiness and preparation for our eternal hope.

If we retain the historic conclusion of the church that homosexual behaviour is sinful, how might we deal with the pastoral questions central to current concern?

How Should the Church Care for those Engaged in Homosexual Activity?

The simple aphorism 'love the sinner, hate the sin' has summed up one traditional way of dealing with sinful behaviour.[27] Perhaps a better expression, which emphasizes the communal and progressive nature of the life of holiness, would be: 'love one another as sinners, help one another not to sin.'

The distinction between tendency and practice remains important. It is roughly parallel to that between temptation and sin. Like temptation any tendency to sinful behaviour is morally ambiguous. It is not sin, but it is a weakness to be

---

27 It has been argued by some in the gay community that such a distinction between practice and orientation cannot be made so simply. But this assumes both that sexual orientation is fundamental to human identity and that a givenness of sexuality takes priority over the givenness of God's word in Scripture. For a recent discussion see D Leal, *Debating Homosexuality* (Grove Ethical Studies 101, Cambridge: Grove Books, 1996).

faced and grappled with, not justified and indulged.[28] The task of separating any sinner from habitual sin is never easy. We cling to our own vices as firmly as a child does to its favourite comfort-blanket. Being sinners means being self-deluded, more easily aware of others' specks than our own beams. Only members of the church who heed the call to holiness and lay themselves open to the exhortation and correction of fellow-believers can earn the right to discipline others. Only a truly holy person can speak easily. Often a truly holy person has no need to speak at all. The challenge to address one kind of sinful behaviour is the challenge to the whole church to be holy and Christ-like, with a common call to compare ourselves only and always with a holy Lord, like us in all things but sin.

Pastoral strategies that focus on the exclusion and silencing of those who engage in homosexual behaviour risk driving people underground, into resistant subcultures or sectarian 'churches.' The impression of transformed community may be easier to maintain but the tough task of demonstrating the transforming power of Jesus Christ in hard cases can too easily be avoided. Pastoral strategies that focus on inclusion and acceptance may provide an easier 'ramp' into the church but they risk compromising its ethical integrity.

An integrated approach requires both that the church stands clearly for its historic convictions through its teaching and discipline, whilst offering the open hand of friendship and love to those struggling with us to obey the truth. A clear view on the ethical question of homosexual behaviour may make it easier for the church to offer love and acceptance because it will not feel itself in danger of ethical compromise. In the context of prayer, fellowship and mutual study of the Scriptures, Christians who are practising homosexuals can be led to conformity—not to social mores, but to the will of God expressed in the Bible.[29]

None of this demands 'instant perfection in the sexual area.'[30] What it does imply is an increasing desire and effort to bring sexual life—as with domestic, economic, social and political life—under the lordship of Christ. Forbidden sexual activity—that which does not correspond to the pattern of Scripture as explored above—needs to be recognized and repented of as do greed, exploitation, unrighteous anger, gossip and all other sins.

An important contribution can be made through the rehabilitation of friendships between persons of the same sex. Warm companionship without any sexual element is not something that should be regarded as odd by the Christian community. Rather it is to be welcomed as a valuable way of developing affectionate bonds within the church and providing the human support and comfort which most of us find we need. However, if everything is related to sexual

28 This point is well made by David Atkinson: 'A distinction between sin and temptation would help many homosexual people rid themselves of a burden of needless guilt.'—*Pastoral Ethics* (Lynx Communications, Oxford 1994).

29 Some writers argue that their sexuality is such an integral part of their personal make up that change is neither possible nor desirable. Others are confident that, despite the difficulties, change is possible—see M Hallett, *I am Learning to Love* (Marshall Pickering, 1987).

30 Vasey, p 59.

identity and activity it becomes increasingly difficult for such friendships to flourish.[31]

How Can the Church Reach Gay and Lesbian People?

Many fear that if the church trumpets its historic teaching on homosexuality too loudly many gays and lesbians who are otherwise attracted to Christ will be put off by the church. But the church approaches any potential believer with nothing other than the good news about Christ, his offer of grace and forgiveness and the transformation of life that is possible and necessary for all of us to enter the kingdom. It is a message full of faith, hope and love but it is also a high calling to endurance, transformation and holiness. We do no justice to Christ or his gospel if we fail to live out its benefits or water down its demands.

The challenge to the church is to be a transformed and transforming community that calls people to the focus of its life and hope in Christ and shows and helps all who come to find the grace and strength to become all that God call them to be. Ultimately we do unrepentant sinners no service by giving admission to the church when God declares that they shall have no part in the kingdom.

The church must also be clear on the subject of prejudice against those of homosexual orientation. Many in the church and society still maintain a deeply-rooted antagonism towards homosexuals which issues in confrontation and violence. Some leaders in the church are given to vituperative and condemnatory public statements. The church should have nothing to do with antagonism and prejudice that condemns rather than helps those struggling with this issue.

Those who are honest about their sexuality, on whichever side of the debate, should not be used as pawns in the discussion over the success or otherwise of different pastoral approaches. Every effort must be made to defend the dignity of individuals and respect the integrity of those with whom we may disagree.

Should Gay People be Ordained?

Discussion of the ordination of homosexuals centres around two issues. Should practising homosexuals be ordained? Should different standards be expected of ordained and lay?[32] This is a question of ecclesiology as well as ethics. The 1991 statement by the House of Bishops of the Church of England argues on both theological and pragmatic grounds that there is no place for clergy 'entering into sexually active homophile relationships.' It also argues that non-ordained gay people

---

31 An increasingly common pattern in both student and young professional circles is for men and women to share a household. In Christian circles this is part of a process of sharing fellowship in a domestic and every day setting and should not be seen as sexual in orientation. This applies also to women sharing with women and men sharing with men.

32 The 'higher' the view of ordination the more easy it is to make distinctions between clergy and laity. As non-stipendiary and recognised lay forms of ministry become increasingly prevalent the distinction between lay and ordained becomes less easy to define.

   The root of the problem is that 'ordination' as now understood (in all its complexity!) is not clearly present in the NT. 1 Tim 4.14 and 2 Tim 1.6-7 speak of the laying on of hands, probably echoing Deut 34.9 but nothing is said of the specific circumstances. See the useful discussion in G Knight III, *The Pastoral Epistles* (NICNT, Eerdmans, 1992) pp 208-9.

can be affirmed in a loving homophile relationship. The biblical view is that leaders (ordained or not) are to be role models of the godly life.

In the pastoral letters a high standard is expected of Christian leaders (1 Tim 3.1-7; 4.12: 'set the believers an example'). Nevertheless it is not a different standard of conduct but the same high standard to which all Christians are called. Leaders are to exemplify and embody a holy and mature Christian life. Their good model in no way excuses others the task of resisting sin. To differentiate sharply between the behaviour expected of lay people and clergy is too easily to give the impression that some Christians are free to sin.

Should practising homosexuals be ordained? Only sinful people can be ordained, otherwise there would be no ordinands and no one to teach them. Grace means we accept our fellow Christians, leaders or not, as forgiven sinners being transformed by the grace of God. But grace is also given to lead to lives of holiness. Of course people guilty of sexual sins can be ordained, as can people guilty of economic, domestic, personality-related and other sins. The biblical call, however, is to renounce and resist such sins and by the grace of God to live differently. Ephesians 4.28 ('let the thief no longer steal') is an example of the profound change grace effects in people's lives.

People of homosexual orientation can be ordained, but are called to lives of holiness. Similarly people with very strong urges in other sexual and non-sexual directions can be ordained, if such urges are resisted by the power of grace. A 'don't ask, don't tell' policy is no way for the church to proceed with integrity. Those continuing in recognized ministry should be expected to live up to their high calling. (And of course the same kind of integrity should be expected of those training for ministry.) Occasional lapses are the subject of the penitential discipline of repentance, forgiveness and restoration. Regular, habitual or wilful failings are not acceptable in leaders. Such behaviour may not appear to affect the substance of ministry but it erodes the trust on which its long-term effectiveness is grounded. It undermines the basic responsibility of ministers not only to teach the faith but to embody and exemplify it for those for whom they care.

How Should Discussion of the Issue of Homosexuality be Conducted?

The debate about homosexual behaviour in the church has to be conducted with a view to the nature of the participants and the context and tone of the debate. Liberation hermeneutics has brought to the attention of the church the question of who has the right to speak. It has pointed out that too often theology had been done 'from above,' not 'from below' and that the situation of the interpreter materially affects interpretative strategy. It is thus argued that exactly the wrong kind of people have been speaking for too long: gays and lesbians have been silenced when they are the only ones who have the right to speak.

The problem with this kind of approach is that it can reduce the authority of the text to the self-interested power-play of the interpreter. If Scripture is God's word then it carries not the authority of self-deluding interpreters but expresses the will and wisdom of God himself. In order to check the possibility of self-delusion on every side the church enters dialogue with those within and beyond the church who can help it to understand and apply Scripture to the realities of human existence. The fact that each participating voice in the discussion is that of a self-deluding sinner calls us to appropriate humility. The fact that we attempt to interpret the word of God means that we can hope to know the truth.

In setting the theological context wider than the Christian community, the church opens itself to constructive dialogue but also wants to assert the rule of God in every area of human existence. It must guard against uncritical dialogue which can easily lead to the secularization of its thinking. The ultimate purpose of dialogue is to come to a theological judgment. Postponement of that judgment should not be used as an excuse for a free-for-all. The burden of proof lies with those who wish to change the historic view of the church and until that point is reached the discipline of the church must be respected. Not to do so is to cause the church prematurely to abandon its position and fail to honour those in the church with homosexual tendencies who have struggled with their sexuality and yet remained celibate.

Other aspects of the way debate has been conducted have been less savoury. Public denunciations and the 'outing' of fellow-Christians are deplorable practices. Attacking the integrity or attempting to ruin the public reputation of another believer will do nothing to advance anyone's case in the minds of godly people. However strongly we feel on an issue we should heed the exhortation to correct with gentleness (2 Tim 2.26). Christ himself advocated the personal touch: 'point out the fault when the two of you are alone...' (Matt 18.15).

Conclusion

Our discussion of gay people in the church is not a call for a witch hunt but for the Christian community to help one another to 'lead a life worthy of the calling to which you have been called.' (Eph 4:1).

There is no suggestion that in sexual matters or in any others that we shall achieve 'instant holiness.' All sexuality is flawed because of the Fall; all of us need repentance and forgiveness. The Titus passage shows the importance of teaching and study of Scripture in the growth in holiness and speaks positively of 'a people of his own who are zealous for good deeds.'

Sexuality, like all other issues, must be seen in an eschatological perspective; 'while we wait for the blessed hope and the manifestation of the glory of our great God and Saviour, Jesus Christ.' The insistence on approval for homosexual activity is part of the obsession with sexuality as the defining and the indispensable condition for human fulfilment. This has in no small measure contributed to the modern church's loss of the vision of heaven as the goal of Christian living. 'For in the resurrection they neither marry nor are given in marriage.' We are on a journey and God calls us to help each other to live in this world in the light of the next. Let us live under grace, helping one another to be faithful to 'him who called us out of darkness into his marvellous light.'